ESCAPING ABUSE STUDY GUIDE

By Glynda Lomax

Escaping Abuse Study Guide

Escaping Abuse Study Guide

By Glynda Lomax

ISBN-13: 978-1983450884

See the author's latest at http://wingsofprophecy.blogspot.com

Online videos available at www.youtube.com/user/texasauthor1

Scripture quotations from The Authorized (King James) Version, unless otherwise noted. Rights in the Authorized Version in the United Kingdom are vested in the Crown. Reproduced by permission of the Crown's patentee, Cambridge University Press.

A liturgical work.

Printed in the United States of America

Abuse always breaks your heart.

CONTENTS

Escaping Abuse Study Guide

HOW ABUSE BEGINS IN THE MIND

Abuse, like every other sin, first begins in the mind. It begins in the mind not only of the abuser, but the mind of the victim. It begins when we see it around us, as small children.

We learn what relationships are supposed to be like by observing the relationships around us as we are growing up. We are taught our parents know best, so their relationship becomes our subconscious model. Our brains process subconscious cues as well as conscious ones, and assimilate all the information into a model in our subconscious for how we should treat others and how we should be treated.

When the Curse of Abuse is on your life, you will usually be able to look back on your childhood and see abuse there. (Not everyone will, and sometimes our subconscious has hidden the memories of these traumas in order for our sanity to survive) It is common to see years of sexual, verbal, emotional, or physical abuse throughout childhood before becoming a victim of domestic violence and other forms of abuse in adulthood.

Often, abuse first begins peeking out in the little things. The disregarding of the feelings of others, small hostilities toward the opposite sex, little underhanded put-downs that demean you, but in a passive-aggressive way you feel but cannot quite put a finger on. Slowly, it becomes stronger, pushing you down, lifting them up ... and then it becomes jealous and controlling. They demand to know where you have been, who you were with. You are accused over and over of things you never so much as thought of doing, ugly name-calling begins, anger rules. You are interrogated for hours over groundless accusations. Accused of being interested in people you did not even look at ...

One day you realize you are trapped in a nightmare of fear and you are helpless to escape. You are imprisoned but only you and the abuser can see the bars that hold you – they will hunt you down and kill you, they will take your children and hide them from you, they will kill your family. You, alone, know they actually are capable of doing these terrible things. You alone have seen the murder in their eyes when they say them. You know they mean it. It is safer to stay than to run.

So you live in your invisible cage and do as you are told, even as you long to be free. Even as you long to be loved – really loved, by someone who is kind, someone who does not scream in your face and leave bruises all over you. Someone you don't have to fear. You long to just be ... normal.

You know another beating is coming, you just don't know when. You are filled with fear every minute of every day. There is no escape. There is only dread. The dread increases as you see their stress level rise. You know what it means, you know what is coming. How bad will it be this time? How bad will you be punished? Will they break bones that will require a doctor's care? What did you ever do to deserve this nightmare of a life you are living?

Someone please help me!

But you can't tell anyone, because they will explode if you do. On you. On the kids. On the pets. On the house.... Involving other people means risking their lives as well as your own ... If only you had some hope of escaping the nightmare that has become your life ...

You long to shout back at their terrible words, but you know better. The price is too high for saying what you really think. Sometimes a few words slip out, and the price you pay is a dear one. Better to just keep quiet. Walk on eggshells and hope for another night of not being hit ...

It's safer just to take it.

Escaping Abuse Study Guide

1. When you look back at your childhood, what kinds of abuse do you see there?

_____

_____

_____

2. In your most recent relationship, in what small ways did abuse begin peeking out?

_____

_____

_____

3. Describe the events you can see abuse in now

_____

_____

_____

_____

_____

4. Have you ever said what you really thought and then paid dearly for it?

_____

What happened?

_____

_____

THE FOUR PHASES LEADING INTO ABUSE

My knowledge of abuse came out of a 12-year abusive marriage, followed by a stay at a domestic violence women's shelter, and later volunteering at a women's shelter in the Dallas, Texas area.There had been some abuse in my family, although I did not recognize it until many years later, when the Lord began to reveal the Curse of Abuse to me.

In considering the abuse I suffered as I encountered other women who had been victims, I discovered strikingsimilarities in the stories of all of us. I began seeing definite patterns. I had read secular books explaining the psychology behind abuse, but as I observed for myself after I was saved and prayed about what I saw and heard, the Lord began to teach me Himself.

In my observations and meditating upon what I saw and heard, I saw four phases that seemed to take place repeatedly as the abuser and victim began to culminate into the life-altering dance of abuse. I am unsure whether the abuser goes through these steps consciously or subconsciously.

I cannot say it is the same for every victim, but I observed it so continually, I can surely say these steps lead the way for many, if not most of them.

1. ISOLATION

I married Rick at the age of 15, so I was a child bride. Rick was 5 years older and on his own forthe first time in his young life. He had left the St. Louis area and come to the Texas Gulf Coast, where we met.

We fell deeply in love and were married about 6 months later. I got pregnant soon after. At the time, Rick worked at a gas filling station on Galveston Island. We did not have enough money and there was great pressure on him to find a way to provide for us. Neither of us came from money, so there was no place to turn for help. It was sink or swim for us.

He began moving us north – first to Canadian, in the panhandle of Texas, where we stayed briefly with my sister, Judy, and her husband, Tom. I remember Rick going to work each day and I would stay in the place we had rented, wondering what to do with myself. I remember trying to learn to shop for groceries on not enough money. I knew Rick needed meat because he had to work, so to make the money stretch, I would pretend not to want any meat and I would eat oatmeal for dinner instead. I remember once I made pork chops for him, and I wanted one of those pork chops so bad, but there just was not enough money for us to have meat all week if I ate meat every dinner with him. He had to go out and work and I knew he needed strength for that. It made the grocery money go further. Soon, we moved again. This time to Elk City, where we stayed briefly with my other sister, Shirley, and her husband William.

Rick and I both got jobs in Elk City. Soon, we took on second jobs. I worked as a waitress and alsoworked cleaning rooms at a motel. I can't remember where Rick's first job was, but he had a second job at Western Auto. We soon rented a small walk-up apartment overlooking the Main Street in town. I was very lonely, spending all my time working or with him, and watching my belly grow. Soon, Rick began to talk of moving further north – towards his home and family, and away from mine.

In about 7 months, we were living in his old family home in East St. Louis, where the abuse he said he witnessed as a child occurred. Not being saved, I had no idea of the spiritual consequences of living in that house. Now I realize the Spirit of Abuse and other spirits such as violence, rape and hatred were in that house with us. The abuse began while we lived there. If the stories Rick told me were true, and I had no reason to believe they weren't, then the abuse was clearly generational, though I knew nothing of generational issues then.

I missed my Mom and my little brother desperately. I had never spent much time away from them. I seldom even spent the night with a friend growing up. The three of us were very tight. Rick and I were desperately poor, living on assistance because we had no vehicle so Rick had no way to get a job and get back and forth to it, and we could barely even buy a few postage stamps each month for me to write to my family. I felt very alone there, with no one around but Rick's family and his friends. His family were not unkind to me, but they all had their own lives and probably wondered what my handsome husband was doing with a plain looking 16 year-old from Texas.

One of my sisters-in-law, Jo, was so nice to me. She gave me two pairs of jeans. I had never had any jeans before and I was so happy to have something nice to wear. She was like an angel of mercy to me during one of the darkest times in my life.

2. ELIMINATION OF RESOURCES

Whatever financial assets or money you have, the abuser will encourage you to spend them on this or that, or will do it for you, and whatever assets you have, they will suggest you sell, or trade in on something else "for the two of you together." This may include houses, lands, vehicles, jewelry, or anything else of value. Basically anything that is worth any money will need to be disposed of in some fashion. The abuser's goal in doing this is to render you without the resources to leave them.

3. THE MENTAL TEAR-DOWN

Once the resources are gone and you are isolated from your own support network, the mental tear-down begins, and the abuser will begin to batter you mentally and emotionally. They will attempt to strip away any self-esteem you had previously, if you had it. In my case, I really didn't have much to begin with, but the tiny speck I had was quickly done away with.

The goal of the mental tear-down is to strip away your confidence to leave them. If they can make you believe no one else will ever want you, that you are lucky to have them, that you are, after all, unattractive, and not at all desirable, then surely you will be grateful to be with them, and stay, regardless of how you are treated.

Now you have no support network, no money or assets, and no self-esteem. You are primed to be the target of physical abuse, and the abuser need not fear you will leave them.

4. THE PHYSICAL ABUSE

At this point, the abuser will usually begin abusing you physically. Often it starts with slapping, shoving, or just throwing things at you. Eventually, it escalates into all-out beatings, choking, slamming you into furniture or cabinetry, and sexually abusing you by forcing unwanted sexual acts on you or forcing you to perform sexual acts you don't want to perform, usually accompanied by name-calling, put-downs and hitting. I have even heard of abusers who force their victims to have unwanted physical relations with others.

Escaping Abuse Study Guide

1. What are the four phases leading into abuse?

_____

_____

_____

_____

2. What thoughts went through your mind that first time you were abused?

_____

_____

_____

3. What excuses did you make for the abuser's behavior?

_____

_____

_____

4. Do you believe God wants you to be abused?

_____

_____

_____

Explain why you believe that

_____

_____

_____

_____

DEFINING ABUSE

There are many ways someone can abuse you. Abuse is at its base line, the wrong use or exploitation of something or someone.

PHYSICAL ABUSE

Probably the most commonly recognized form of abuse is physical abuse, commonly called Domestic Violence. In recent years, much awareness of domestic violence has permeated the media, especially as various celebrities and sports figures have been in the news linked to it.

To abuse means to use wrongly. People were not created by a loving God to be punching bags or sex abuse objects. He did not create you so someone else could push, shove, pinch or slap on you. That is wrong use.

Some people believe unless you land a full-fisted blow into someone's face that you did not abuse them. That is incorrect. Abuse is any wrong use of something or someone.

If you pushed, shoved, pinched, slapped, forced sex on, withheld money from, engaged in name-calling of, emotionally blackmailed, or did a number of other wrong things to someone, then you abused them. And if you yourself have suffered these things, then you have also been abused. It is no fun being on either side of the Curse of Abuse.

Whether you are an abuser, a victim, or you just have a friend or family member who is, it is no fun. The good news is, everyone involved in abuse can break free of this horrible curse.

God desires that we all be free of abuse and of being abusive to others.

VERBAL ABUSE

One of the most common types of abuse anywhere is verbal abuse. What is verbal abuse?

To abuse someone verbally is to yell at them, to call them names, to belittle them, call them stupid, ugly, void of common sense, worthless, fat, or any one of a million other derogatory names and curse words.

Verbal abuse is basically hitting someone with the power of ugly words instead of hitting them with a fist. It is bruising them on the inside. The effect is devastating, and long lasting.

Threatening is another form of verbal abuse. Intimidation is always a part of domestic abuse, and abusers intimidate their victims in numerous ways – they withhold finances, threaten bodily harm, threaten the loss of children or custody of children, threaten to harm the pets, threaten to harm the victim's family members, threaten to ruin reputations and businesses, financial security, and more.

Abuse is terrorism practiced in the home. It is manipulating and controlling someone by using physical violence, terror and intimidation.

Verbal abuse is not taken as seriously as physical abuse, but it is very serious, and very damaging, especially if it goes on for years. As it goes on and on and on, the victim is in danger of believing the lies the abuser is feeding him or her.

SEXUAL ABUSE

One of the worst forms of abuse is sexual abuse. I will not go into a lot of detail about this kind of abuse, but every abused woman I have ever met has been through it. This form of abuse is the most difficult to heal from of all.

Bruises heal after you take a beating, but sexual abuse leaves a much deeper wound on your soul. Rape is a form of punishment, and in domestic violence, it is done in the most painful and degrading ways possible, and is always accompanied by verbal abuse – cursing, name-calling, and sometimes physical abuse as well.

FINANCIAL ABUSE

Financial abuse is a type of abuse practiced by withholding needed finances, financial assets or access to financial accounts in order to control and punish another person.

Withholding grocery money or funds to pay utilities on time causes the other party pain and anguish, and worse, and is used to punish them for imagined wrongs.

Withholding access to financial accounts and assets is also a way to keep you deprived of the resources needed to leave the abuser.

LEGAL ABUSE

Legal abuse is a way to deplete a victim's finances while also depleting their time. It is often practiced by filing frivolous motions or lawsuits repeatedly, causing the abused party to deplete their finances in order to defend themselves in court.

STALKING VIA CONSTANTLY CONTACTING YOU

Constantly keeping tabs on someone via repeated phone calls, constantly texting, etc. is also abuse. This is a form of stalking, and it is used to exercise control over where the victim is and who they are with.

Escaping Abuse Study Guide

1. The most commonly recognized form of abuse is _____ abuse.

2. Verbal abuse is hitting someone with the power of _____ _____ instead of hitting them with a fist. It is bruising them on the _____.

3. Abuse is _____ practiced in the home.

4. _____ abuse is not taken as seriously as physical abuse, but it is very serious, and very damaging. As it goes on and on, the victim is in danger of _____ the _____ the abuser is feeding him or her.

5. The most difficult form of abuse to heal from is _____ abuse.

6. _____ is a form of punishment.

7. Withholding access to _____ _____ and _____ is also a way to keep you deprived of the resources needed to leave the abuser.

8. Filing frivolous motions or lawsuits is called _____ abuse.

9. Constantly contacting you via phone or text is a form of _____.

10. Describe a time when you were physically abused.

_____
_____
_____
_____
_____

11. Describe a time you remember well when you were verbally abused

_____
_____
_____
_____
_____

12. Did you ever witness abuse when you were a child

_____
_____
_____
_____
_____

13. Are other members of your family abusers or abuse victims?

_____
_____

Have you witnessed the abuse?

_____
_____
_____

14. Are any members of your partner's family abusers or abuse victims?

_____

_____

Have you witnessed any abuse among them?

_____

_____

_____

15. Name one thing your abuser convinced you of that you never believed before the abuse?

_____

_____

_____

_____

_____

16. How many types of abuse can you name?

_____

_____

_____

_____

_____

THE REVELATION OF THE CURSE OF ABUSE

It was near the end of September 2012, and autumn was in the air in North Texas. Soft September breezes blew the autumn-hued leaves in swirling dances along the ground as the blazing Texas summer quietly began surrendering to fall.

For weeks, I had been studying and sharing a series on spiritual warfare and breaking generational curses on Blog Talk Radio. On this morning, I was sitting on my bed with reference books in piles all around me, making notes for my next show.

Sitting there on the bed, I was talking to the Lord about something to do with warfare, asking Him what kinds of curses could pass generationally – was it just certain sins, or was it all of them? I needed to understand in order not to pass wrong information on to my listeners on Blog Talk Radio. Suddenly, a vision opened up in my spirit.

In my spirit, I was shown there was a generational Curse of Abuse on my family. I had heard of generational curses, but I had never a Curse of Abuse. I sat on my bed in silent shock as the Lord revealed more to me. My Dad did not beat on my Mom, so I was baffled by what I was shown. I have since realized though he did not hit her, he did abuse her in other ways.

In my spirit, I was shown my parents, and each of my siblings, and how the curse had manifested in each of their lives. He didn't need to show me mine, I already knew how it had manifested for me.

I grew up in a barely functioning family with one alcoholic parent, and constant bickering and strife. Verbal abuse was rampant in our home, and though Mom caught the brunt of it, we children were not immune, either. I had survived over ten years of sexual abuse in childhood as well, and then married into more abuse.

Abuse was a subject I was more than a little bit familiar with. I knew far more about it than I had ever wanted to learn, but I had no idea it was or could be a curse.

Over the following weeks and months, He continued to reveal to me how the enemy uses assignments of abuse to delay and even derail the destinies of His children. I began to study it in more depth. At times shocked, horrified and saddened by what I discovered, I determined to share what He had showed me that others might find their way free from this terrible curse.

This Study Guide is the result of the revelation the Lord gave me about my own family, the studying I have done and what I know from years of practicing spiritual warfare. It is my prayer it will help you to get free from any abuse in your own life. The Lord desires His people to be free of the enemy's snares and traps, but we can only get free if we know what traps we are caught in.

For years I had worked diligently to help others get free of addictions, lawlessness, perversion and depression by sharing what I knew about casting out the spirits that bound them, only to see the spirits come back, again and again.

What am I doing wrong, Lord? Why can I not get them free? Are they getting free and going back to the sin or is it something I'm doing wrong? I want so much to see them get free!

What I learned as I kept studying is that a curse is like the Strongman that must be bound (only in the case of a curse, you break it instead of binding it) before you can cast out the demons and make them stay gone. Otherwise, they have a legal right to come right back in.

The curse operates like an open door.

BUT WAIT – DIDN'T JESUS BECOME A CURSE FOR US?

In order to understand curses, you must first realize the spiritual realm, though most cannot see it, is very real. Jesus saw it, and dealt with it. Most churches today do not do as Jesus did in this regard, and their congregations continue struggling, many remaining bound by the forces and curses they cannot see.

GALATIANS 3:13

13 CHRIST HATH REDEEMED US FROM THE CURSE OF THE LAW, BEING MADE A CURSE FOR US: FOR IT IS WRITTEN, CURSED IS EVERY ONE THAT HANGETH ON A TREE:

Most people assume that because Jesus became a curse for us, that we cannot be under a curse any longer if we are saved.

1 PETER 3:18

18 FOR CHRIST ALSO HATH ONCE SUFFERED FOR SINS, THE JUST FOR THE UNJUST, THAT HE MIGHT BRING US TO GOD, BEING PUT TO DEATH IN THE FLESH, BUT QUICKENED BY THE SPIRIT:

Jesus also died for everyone's sins. Is everyone free of sin? No. Why not?

Because everyone has not appropriated what Jesus did for them and renewed their minds in His Word to overcome their sin.

JOHN 3:16

16 FOR GOD SO LOVED THE WORLD, THAT HE GAVE HIS ONLY BEGOTTEN SON, THAT WHOSOEVER BELIEVETH IN HIM SHOULD NOT PERISH, BUT HAVE EVERLASTING LIFE.

Jesus died that we might all be saved. So why is everyone not saved then? Because everyone has not appropriated what Jesus did for them in their own lives.

So even though Jesus did become a curse for us when He hung on the cross, what He so graciously did for us will not help us be free of all the curses *unless we appropriate it*. The purpose of this Study Guide is to help you learn how to appropriate what He did so you can be free of the Curse of Abuse.

EVIL IN THE UNSEEN REALM

In the spiritual realm that we cannot see, there are evil forces at work against you and all those you love. Every single day. They whisper lies, trying to deceive you, lead you astray and bring as much destruction and havoc into your life as they can.

How much destruction these forces bring, and to what extent they are able to destroy, depends on you.

There is only one way to stop these demonic forces from their destructive work in your life, and that is by the power of the shed Blood of Jesus Christ. The Blood of Christ can be wielded by every believer who is willing to pick up the Sword of the Word of God and fight back.

If you have not given your heart and life to Jesus, this Study Guide will give you information about why you do the things you do, but not the authority to change it. However, if you will give Him a chance to change your life for the better, He will, and you will receive not only the authority to make these changes, but eternal life with Him as well.

The choice is yours.

I spent three and a half decades as an unsaved person before I found Jesus and surrendered control of my life to Him. In those years, I suffered many devastating blows from the demons. My children suffered, my then-spouse suffered. My family suffered. None of us knew where the bad was coming from, or how to stop it then.

Since giving Him my life, I walk in constant peace. I have the authority to stop those evil forces in their tracks, and you can, too.

If you want to surrender your life to Jesus, all you have to do is believe He is who He says He is, and tell Him so.

If you want to give your life to the Lord, just say this prayer:

Lord Jesus, I'm tired of going my own way now and I would like to try Yours. I give you my heart and my life. I do believe you are the living Son of God, and that You died on the cross at Calvary for my sins. I believe Father God raised You from the dead and You now sit at His right hand in heaven. Come into my heart and help me start anew. Help me to do what I need to do, Lord. I need You. Amen.

Escaping Abuse Study Guide

1. The curse operates like an _____ _____.

2. Have you ever cast out demons before and had them come right back?

_____

3. What Jesus did for us at the cross will not help us be free of all the curses unless we _____ it.

4. Why is everyone not free of sin?

_____

_____

_____

_____

_____

_____

_____

5. The only way to stop the demonic forces from their destructive work in your life is through the power of the _____

_____ of _____ _____ .

HAVE YOU EVER WONDERED WHY YOU BEHAVE THE WAY YOU DO?

Have you ever wondered why you do the things you do? Why you abuse others or tolerate abuse from others? Why you do things you know better than to do? Do you ever feel as if there is a driving force pushing you to do these things?

There actually are such forces in the unseen realm around you and those forces influence humans every day to do things, both good and bad. Evil or demonic spirits influence us to do bad, angels influence us to do good.

EXODUS 20:5

5 THOU SHALT NOT BOW DOWN THYSELF TO THEM, NOR SERVE THEM: FOR I THE LORD THY GOD AM A JEALOUS GOD, VISITING THE INIQUITY OF THE FATHERS UPON THE CHILDREN UNTO THE THIRD AND FOURTH GENERATION OF THEM THAT HATE ME;

WHAT IS INIQUITY?

Iniquity is a word found throughout scripture; it often refers to the state of being crooked, bent or perverse. So in other words, a state of being twisted or crooked or doing things in a twisted, perverse or crooked way, as shown in the scripture referring to Sodom and Gomorrah:

GENESIS 19:15

15 AND WHEN THE MORNING AROSE, THEN THE ANGELS HASTENED LOT, SAYING, ARISE, TAKE THY WIFE, AND THY TWO DAUGHTERS, WHICH ARE HERE; LEST THOU BE CONSUMED IN THE INIQUITY OF THE CITY.

Iniquity is another name for sin that is passed down from one generation to the next through the male bloodline. These sins often fall under the name "generational curses." Abuse is most often passed through a generational curse on the male bloodline.

There are many types of sin that can be passed to us through generational curses. This Study Guide will focus mainly on sins having to do with abuse, but all generational curses work pretty much the same way.

Escaping Abuse Study Guide

1. Iniquity is a state of being _____ or _____,
or doing things in a _____, _____
or _____ way, as shown in the scripture referring
to Sodom and Gomorrah.

2. Iniquity is another name for sin that is passed down from one
generation to the next through the _____
_____.

3. Abuse is most often passed through a _____
_____ on the male bloodline.

4. Did you ever think growing up that you would become part of
an abusive relationship?

_____

_____

_____

5. What has life been like for you in your most recent
relationship?

_____

_____

_____

_____

_____

_____

TO DEAL WITH CURSES, YOU MUST KNOW ABOUT DEMONS

WHERE DO DEMONS COME FROM?

There are several theories about where demons come from. Since our best information about the truth of any matter is always going to be the Word of God, let's look there.

We cannot say exactly when angels were created. However, we can make some other general deductions based on what we know from the Bible.

Scripture reveals that demons (also called 'devils') are <u>directly connected to Satan</u> (Matt. 12:24-26; 25:41; Luke 10:17-20; Rev. 12:7).

MATTHEW 12:24-26

24 BUT WHEN THE PHARISEES HEARD IT, THEY SAID, THIS FELLOW DOTH NOT CAST OUT DEVILS, BUT BY BEELZEBUB THE PRINCE OF THE DEVILS.

25 AND JESUS KNEW THEIR THOUGHTS, AND SAID UNTO THEM, EVERY KINGDOM DIVIDED AGAINST ITSELF IS BROUGHT TO DESOLATION; AND EVERY CITY OR HOUSE DIVIDED AGAINST ITSELF SHALL NOT STAND:

26 AND IF SATAN CAST OUT SATAN, HE IS DIVIDED AGAINST HIMSELF; HOW SHALL THEN HIS KINGDOM STAND?

MATTHEW 25:41

41 THEN SHALL HE SAY ALSO UNTO THEM ON THE LEFT HAND, DEPART FROM ME, YE CURSED, INTO EVERLASTING FIRE, PREPARED FOR THE DEVIL AND HIS ANGELS:

LUKE 10:17-20

17 AND THE SEVENTY RETURNED AGAIN WITH JOY, SAYING, LORD, EVEN THE DEVILS ARE SUBJECT UNTO US THROUGH THY NAME.

18 AND HE SAID UNTO THEM, I BEHELD SATAN AS LIGHTNING FALL FROM HEAVEN.

19 BEHOLD, I GIVE UNTO YOU POWER TO TREAD ON SERPENTS AND SCORPIONS, AND OVER ALL THE POWER OF THE ENEMY: AND NOTHING SHALL BY ANY MEANS HURT YOU.

20 NOTWITHSTANDING IN THIS REJOICE NOT, THAT THE SPIRITS ARE SUBJECT UNTO YOU; BUT RATHER REJOICE, BECAUSE YOUR NAMES ARE WRITTEN IN HEAVEN.

REVELATION 12:7

7 AND THERE WAS WAR IN HEAVEN: MICHAEL AND HIS ANGELS FOUGHT AGAINST THE DRAGON; AND THE DRAGON FOUGHT AND HIS ANGELS,

Since Michael and his angels fought against the dragon (the dragon is Satan) and the dragon fought and his angels, it appears these angels (also called 'spirits' and 'unclean spirits') fell at the same time Satan did by joining him in his rebellion against God, which apparently occurred before the fall of Adam and Eve in Eden since Satan was the serpent that deceived Eve there.

GENESIS 3:1

1 NOW THE SERPENT WAS MORE SUBTIL THAN ANY BEAST OF THE FIELD WHICH THE LORD GOD HAD MADE. AND HE SAID UNTO THE WOMAN, YEA, HATH GOD SAID, YE SHALL NOT EAT OF EVERY TREE OF THE GARDEN?

MATTHEW 17:18

18 AND JESUS REBUKED THE DEVIL; AND HE DEPARTED OUT OF HIM: AND THE CHILD WAS CURED FROM THAT VERY HOUR.

REVELATION 20:2

2 AND HE LAID HOLD ON THE DRAGON, THAT OLD SERPENT, WHICH IS THE DEVIL, AND SATAN, AND BOUND HIM A THOUSAND YEARS,

MATTHEW 25:41

41 THEN SHALL HE SAY ALSO UNTO THEM ON THE LEFT HAND, DEPART FROM ME, YE CURSED, INTO EVERLASTING FIRE, PREPARED FOR THE DEVIL AND HIS ANGELS:

How many angels fell in the rebellion and became demons? We don't know. The first part of Revelations 12:4 gives us a clue to how many angels fell from heaven.

REVELATION 12:4

4 AND HIS TAIL DREW THE THIRD PART OF THE STARS OF HEAVEN, AND DID CAST THEM TO THE EARTH: AND THE DRAGON STOOD BEFORE THE WOMAN WHICH WAS READY TO BE DELIVERED, FOR TO DEVOUR HER CHILD AS SOON AS IT WAS BORN.

There are myriads – millions and perhaps billions or even trillions of angels. A third of a number like that would be a considerable amount, to be sure.

To sum up, God created all the angels perfect and holy (of which Lucifer, now Satan, was once one), and we don't know how many the Lord God created. Some of them apparently were seduced by Lucifer into disbelieving and disobeying God and became part of the rebellion that got Lucifer cast out of heaven. They were cast out and given over to wickedness – they had no part in God anymore, so all that was left was to be evil.

So it appears from scripture demons may have been holy angels who got kicked out of heaven for acting badly (rebelling against

God) and they are now someplace else, no longer serving God, but the devil.

MATTHEW 25:41

41 THEN SHALL HE SAY ALSO UNTO THEM ON THE LEFT HAND, DEPART FROM ME, YE CURSED, INTO EVERLASTING FIRE, PREPARED FOR THE DEVIL AND HIS ANGELS:

REVELATION 12:9

9 AND THE GREAT DRAGON WAS CAST OUT, THAT OLD SERPENT, CALLED THE DEVIL, AND SATAN, WHICH DECEIVETH THE WHOLE WORLD: HE WAS CAST OUT INTO THE EARTH, AND HIS ANGELS WERE CAST OUT WITH HIM.

A second theory is that demons are a pre-Adamic race. A third theory is that they are the spirits left behind by the race of offspringcreated when the giants mated with women.

1. There are several theories about where _____ come from.

2. And the great dragon was cast out, that old _____, called the _____, and _____, which deceiveth the whole world: he was cast out into the earth, and his angels were cast out with him.

3. Scripture reveals that demons are directly connected to _____.

4. The everlasting fire was prepared for the _____ and his _____.

5. Our best information about the truth on any matter is always going to be the _____ _____ _____.

6. Write out your favorite verse about power over demons or demonic forces

_____

_____

_____

_____

_____

_____

EVIDENCE SUGGESTS THAT DEMONS ARE FALLEN ANGELS

Scriptural evidence suggests that demons are fallen angels. It stands to reason if demons were originally created angels, they probably have the same type abilities as angels have.

MATTHEW 8:16

16 WHEN THE EVEN WAS COME, THEY BROUGHT UNTO HIM MANY THAT WERE POSSESSED WITH DEVILS: AND HE CAST OUT THE SPIRITS WITH HIS WORD, AND HEALED ALL THAT WERE SICK:

LUKE 10:20

20 NOTWITHSTANDING IN THIS REJOICE NOT, THAT THE SPIRITS ARE SUBJECT UNTO YOU; BUT RATHER REJOICE, BECAUSE YOUR NAMES ARE WRITTEN IN HEAVEN.

MARK 9:25

25 WHEN JESUS SAW THAT THE PEOPLE CAME RUNNING TOGETHER, HE REBUKED THE FOUL SPIRIT, SAYING UNTO HIM, THOU DUMB AND DEAF SPIRIT, I CHARGE THEE, COME OUT OF HIM, AND ENTER NO MORE INTO HIM.

First, as with the holy angels, demons are personal, or maybe a better way of saying it is that they are individual creatures, each with its own personality.

Angels held conversations with humans in many places in the Bible – they bring or teach us things. So it stands to reason that demons also bring or teach us things. Just not good things, where demons are concerned.

Daniel 9:20-24

20 And whiles I was speaking, and praying, and confessing my sin and the sin of my people Israel, and presenting my supplication before the Lord my God for the holy mountain of my God;

21 Yea, whiles I was speaking in prayer, even the man Gabriel, whom I had seen in the vision at the beginning, being caused to fly swiftly, touched me about the time of the evening oblation.

22 And he informed me, and talked with me, and said, O Daniel, I am now come forth to give thee skill and understanding.

23 At the beginning of thy supplications the commandment came forth, and I am come to shew thee; for thou art greatly beloved: therefore understand the matter, and consider the vision.

24 Seventy weeks are determined upon thy people and upon thy holy city, to finish the transgression, and to make an end of sins, and to make reconciliation for iniquity, and to bring in everlasting righteousness, and to seal up the vision and prophecy, and to anoint the most Holy.

Daniel 10:10-12

10 And, behold, an hand touched me, which set me upon my knees and upon the palms of my hands.

11 And he said unto me, O Daniel, a man greatly beloved, understand the words that I speak unto thee, and stand upright: for unto thee am I now sent. And when he had spoken this word unto me, I stood trembling.

12 Then said he unto me, Fear not, Daniel: for from the first day that thou didst set thine heart to understand, and to chasten thyself before thy God, thy words were heard, and I am come for thy words.

Here an angel is seen giving instructions to Joseph to protect Jesus:

MATTHEW 2:11-13

11 AND WHEN THEY WERE COME INTO THE HOUSE, THEY SAW THE YOUNG CHILD WITH MARY HIS MOTHER, AND FELL DOWN, AND WORSHIPPED HIM: AND WHEN THEY HAD OPENED THEIR TREASURES, THEY PRESENTED UNTO HIM GIFTS; GOLD, AND FRANKINCENSE AND MYRRH.

12 AND BEING WARNED OF GOD IN A DREAM THAT THEY SHOULD NOT RETURN TO HEROD, THEY DEPARTED INTO THEIR OWN COUNTRY ANOTHER WAY.

13 AND WHEN THEY WERE DEPARTED, BEHOLD, THE ANGEL OF THE LORD APPEARETH TO JOSEPH IN A DREAM, SAYING, ARISE, AND TAKE THE YOUNG CHILD AND HIS MOTHER, AND FLEE INTO EGYPT, AND BE THOU THERE UNTIL I BRING THEE WORD: FOR HEROD WILL SEEK THE YOUNG CHILD TO DESTROY HIM.

Here angels talked to the women at Jesus' tomb:

MATTHEW 28:1-7

1 IN THE END OF THE SABBATH, AS IT BEGAN TO DAWN TOWARD THE FIRST DAY OF THE WEEK, CAME MARY MAGDALENE AND THE OTHER MARY TO SEE THE SEPULCHRE.

2 AND, BEHOLD, THERE WAS A GREAT EARTHQUAKE: FOR THE ANGEL OF THE LORD DESCENDED FROM HEAVEN, AND CAME AND ROLLED BACK THE STONE FROM THE DOOR, AND SAT UPON IT.

3 HIS COUNTENANCE WAS LIKE LIGHTNING, AND HIS RAIMENT WHITE AS SNOW:

4 AND FOR FEAR OF HIM THE KEEPERS DID SHAKE, AND BECAME AS DEAD MEN.

5 AND THE ANGEL ANSWERED AND SAID UNTO THE WOMEN, FEAR NOT YE: FOR I KNOW THAT YE SEEK JESUS, WHICH WAS CRUCIFIED.

6 HE IS NOT HERE: FOR HE IS RISEN, AS HE SAID. COME, SEE THE PLACE WHERE THE LORD LAY.

7 AND GO QUICKLY, AND TELL HIS DISCIPLES THAT HE IS RISEN FROM THE DEAD; AND, BEHOLD, HE GOETH BEFORE YOU INTO GALILEE; THERE SHALL YE SEE HIM: LO, I HAVE TOLD YOU.

Escaping Abuse Study Guide

1. _____ evidence is that the demons are fallen angels. It stands to reason if demons were originally created angels, they probably have the same type _____ as angels have.

2. _____ talked to the women at Jesus' tomb.

3. Write out your favorite verse about angels

_____

_____

_____

_____

_____

_____

4. Angels hold _____ with humans in many places in the Bible.

5. Demons have a _____ _____ and _____ that they hold to and propagate.

DEMONS HAVE INTELLIGENCE

We can see that demons have intelligence. This is also revealed by the fact that Jesus and others conversed with them on different occasions. (Matthew 8:28-32; Mark 9:25-26, Acts 19:13-15)

MATTHEW 8:28-32

28 AND WHEN HE WAS COME TO THE OTHER SIDE INTO THE COUNTRY OF THE GERGESENES, THERE MET HIM TWO POSSESSED WITH DEVILS, COMING OUT OF THE TOMBS, EXCEEDING FIERCE, SO THAT NO MAN MIGHT PASS BY THAT WAY.

29 AND, BEHOLD, THEY CRIED OUT, SAYING, WHAT HAVE WE TO DO WITH THEE, JESUS, THOU SON OF GOD? ART THOU COME HITHER TO TORMENT US BEFORE THE TIME?

30 AND THERE WAS A GOOD WAY OFF FROM THEM AN HERD OF MANY SWINE FEEDING.

31 SO THE DEVILS BESOUGHT HIM, SAYING, IF THOU CAST US OUT, SUFFER US TO GO AWAY INTO THE HERD OF SWINE.

32 AND HE SAID UNTO THEM, GO. AND WHEN THEY WERE COME OUT, THEY WENT INTO THE HERD OF SWINE: AND, BEHOLD, THE WHOLE HERD OF SWINE RAN VIOLENTLY DOWN A STEEP PLACE INTO THE SEA, AND PERISHED IN THE WATERS.

MARK 9:25-26

25 WHEN JESUS SAW THAT THE PEOPLE CAME RUNNING TOGETHER, HE REBUKED THE FOUL SPIRIT, SAYING UNTO HIM, THOU DUMB AND DEAF SPIRIT, I CHARGE THEE, COME OUT OF HIM, AND ENTER NO MORE INTO HIM.

26 AND THE SPIRIT CRIED, AND RENT HIM SORE, AND CAME OUT OF HIM: AND HE WAS AS ONE DEAD; INSOMUCH THAT MANY SAID, HE IS DEAD.

ACTS 19:13-15

13 THEN CERTAIN OF THE VAGABOND JEWS, EXORCISTS, TOOK UPON THEM TO CALL OVER THEM WHICH HAD EVIL SPIRITS THE NAME OF THE LORD JESUS, SAYING, WE ADJURE YOU BY JESUS WHOM PAUL PREACHETH.

14 AND THERE WERE SEVEN SONS OF ONE SCEVA, A JEW, AND CHIEF OF THE PRIESTS, WHICH DID SO.

15 AND THE EVIL SPIRIT ANSWERED AND SAID, JESUS I KNOW, AND PAUL I KNOW; BUT WHO ARE YE?

Demons have a belief system and doctrine that they hold to and propagate (1 Timothy 4:1-3).

1 TIMOTHY 4:1-3

4 NOW THE SPIRIT SPEAKETH EXPRESSLY, THAT IN THE LATTER TIMES SOME SHALL DEPART FROM THE FAITH, GIVING HEED TO SEDUCING SPIRITS, AND DOCTRINES OF DEVILS;

2 SPEAKING LIES IN HYPOCRISY; HAVING THEIR CONSCIENCE SEARED WITH A HOT IRON;

3 FORBIDDING TO MARRY, AND COMMANDING TO ABSTAIN FROM MEATS, WHICH GOD HATH CREATED TO BE RECEIVED WITH THANKSGIVING OF THEM WHICH BELIEVE AND KNOW THE TRUTH.

As with the angels, their knowledge is no doubt greater than man's for they have access to information that we do not, and they have been around in the world far longer than we have. For instance, the demons possessing the man in Mark 1:23-24 knew exactly who Jesus really was, while the other people in the synagogue at that point had no clue.

MARK 1:23-24

23 AND THERE WAS IN THEIR SYNAGOGUE A MAN WITH AN UNCLEAN SPIRIT; AND HE CRIED OUT,

24 SAYING, LET US ALONE; WHAT HAVE WE TO DO WITH THEE, THOU JESUS OF NAZARETH? ART THOU COME TO DESTROY US? I KNOW THEE WHO THOU ART, THE HOLY ONE OF GOD.

It should be noted, however, that even though demons may know more than we do, they are not omniscient – they do not know everything. This is because they were created by God and are therefore limited. Only God Himself has all knowledge and all power.

The Bible also discloses that demons have emotions. Some of the passages we have looked at show they have a great fear of what Jesus is capable of doing to them. James 2:19 clearly affirms this fact.

JAMES 2:19

19 THOU BELIEVEST THAT THERE IS ONE GOD; THOU DOEST WELL: THE DEVILS ALSO BELIEVE, AND TREMBLE.

Demons also have a will, having followed Satan into rebellion against God. Clearly, they made the choice to do that. The book of Jude also indicates they possess this trait.

JUDE 6

6 AND THE ANGELS WHICH KEPT NOT THEIR FIRST ESTATE, BUT LEFT THEIR OWN HABITATION, HE HATH RESERVED IN EVERLASTING CHAINS UNDER DARKNESS UNTO THE JUDGMENT OF THE GREAT DAY.

Escaping Abuse Study Guide

1. The demons possessing the man in Mark 1:23-24 knew exactly who _____ really was, while the other people in the synagogue at that point had no clue.

2. Demons also have a _____, having followed Satan into rebellion against God.

3. Even though demons may know more than we do, they are not omniscient – they do not know _____.

4. The Bible also discloses that demons have _____.

5._____have a great fear of what Jesus is capable of doing to them. _____ _____ clearly affirms this.

DEMONS HAVE PERSONALITIES AND THEY WANT TO CAUSE HARM

Demons have a sense of self or personal identity. We have already seen examples of how they use personal pronouns ("I, we, us") to refer to themselves. They also have (or take) names, according to Mark 5:6-9.

These four things, intelligence, emotions, volition (will) and sense of self, are the marks of personality.

Mark 5:6-9

6 But when he saw Jesus afar off, he ran and worshipped him,

7 And cried with a loud voice, and said, What have I to do with thee, Jesus, thou Son of the most high God? I adjure thee by God, that thou torment me not.

8 For he said unto him, Come out of the man, thou unclean spirit.

9 And he asked him, What is thy name? And he answered, saying, My name is Legion: for we are many.

Angels are essentially spirits that minister for us (if demons don't minister for us, what do *they* do?)

In scripture, we do not find any identifiable cases where demons were helpful to us or ministering good things to humans. In every instance in the Bible, demons are harming or trying to harm humans.

DEMONS WANT TO HARM YOU

That demons want to cause harm can be deduced by the fact that in almost every instance of demon possession we see in the Bible, the person possessed is being hurt.

MARK 9:25-26

25 WHEN JESUS SAW THAT THE PEOPLE CAME RUNNING TOGETHER, HE REBUKED THE FOUL SPIRIT, SAYING UNTO HIM, THOU DUMB AND DEAF SPIRIT, I CHARGE THEE, COME OUT OF HIM, AND ENTER NO MORE INTO HIM.

26 AND THE SPIRIT CRIED, AND RENT HIM SORE, AND CAME OUT OF HIM: AND HE WAS AS ONE DEAD; INSOMUCH THAT MANY SAID, HE IS DEAD.

ACTS 19:13-16

13 THEN CERTAIN OF THE VAGABOND JEWS, EXORCISTS, TOOK UPON THEM TO CALL OVER THEM WHICH HAD EVIL SPIRITS THE NAME OF THE LORD JESUS, SAYING, WE ADJURE YOU BY JESUS WHOM PAUL PREACHETH.

14 AND THERE WERE SEVEN SONS OF ONE SCEVA, A JEW, AND CHIEF OF THE PRIESTS, WHICH DID SO.

15 AND THE EVIL SPIRIT ANSWERED AND SAID, JESUS I KNOW, AND PAUL I KNOW; BUT WHO ARE YE?

16 AND THE MAN IN WHOM THE EVIL SPIRIT WAS LEAPED ON THEM, AND OVERCAME THEM, AND PREVAILED AGAINST THEM, SO THAT THEY FLED OUT OF THAT HOUSE NAKED AND WOUNDED.

Demons sometimes have considerable power. This is revealed in the tremendous strength they imbue to the people they possess. (Mark 5:2-4, Acts 19:16)

MARK 5:2-4

2 AND WHEN HE WAS COME OUT OF THE SHIP, IMMEDIATELY THERE MET HIM OUT OF THE TOMBS A MAN WITH AN UNCLEAN SPIRIT,

3 WHO HAD HIS DWELLING AMONG THE TOMBS; AND NO MAN COULD BIND HIM, NO, NOT WITH CHAINS:

4 BECAUSE THAT HE HAD BEEN OFTEN BOUND WITH FETTERS AND CHAINS, AND THE CHAINS HAD BEEN PLUCKED ASUNDER BY HIM, AND THE FETTERS BROKEN IN PIECES: NEITHER COULD ANY MAN TAME HIM.

ACTS 19:16

16 AND THE MAN IN WHOM THE EVIL SPIRIT WAS LEAPED ON THEM, AND OVERCAME THEM, AND PREVAILED AGAINST THEM, SO THAT THEY FLED OUT OF THAT HOUSE NAKED AND WOUNDED.

In Revelations we see that demons will be unrestrained for a time and will wreak much destruction by the fact that they will control certain terrible beings (9:10-11; 14-16).

Jesus Himself implied that demons had considerable power in some cases:

MARK 9:28-29

28 AND WHEN HE WAS COME INTO THE HOUSE, HIS DISCIPLES ASKED HIM PRIVATELY, WHY COULD NOT WE CAST HIM OUT?

29 AND HE SAID UNTO THEM, THIS KIND CAN COME FORTH BY NOTHING, BUT BY PRAYER AND FASTING.

As we have seen in many of our passages, any authority they have or activity they pursue is limited to what God allows (cf. Rev. 9:4-5, 14-15). They are neither omnipresent (everywhere at once) nor omnipotent (all powerful). Only God Himself has those characteristics.

We also know that demons are opposed to God. They have an underlying hatred for God and the things and people of God.

Demons work continually to try to destroy anything or anyone that is important to or that resembles God. The simple fact that God loves us so much is why they hate us.

Psalm 91 states that God gives His angels charge over us. The devil attempts to counterfeit every good thing God does, and if God gives His angels charge over us, we have to wonder what Satan is doing with *his* angels regarding us.

1. Demons have a sense of self or personal

_____.

2. These four things,_____, _____,
_____, and _____, are the marks of
personality.

3. In every instance in the Bible, demons are _____ or
trying to _____ humans.

4. Demons sometimes have considerable _____.

5. Any authority they (demons) have or activity they pursue is
limited to what God _____.

6. Because that he had been often bound with fetters and chains,
and the chains had been plucked asunder by him, and the fetters
broken in pieces: neither could any man _____ him.

WE ARE IN A BATTLE

Is the spiritual battle real or imagined?Aren't Christians delivered of demons when they get saved?But Jesus already defeated the enemy!Can a Christian be possessed?Will the Enemy retaliate if I cast out a demon?

There is a great need for teaching about the spiritual realm and our authority over demons. Sin is so prevalent in the world, and churches simply do not have the manpower and enough time to do as much deliverance as is needed in order to get the people free who desire freedom.

Most churches are not equipped to deal with deliverance – it's messy and it can get ugly in some cases, especially if the deliverance team is inexperienced. In a church, deliverance should always be done by a trained team of four to six people, with a designated leader. Most of the time it's fairly calm, but certain demons want to make a big show of it.

Believers need at least a working knowledge of spiritual warfare and curses so they can get themselves free and minister to their family, if nothing else. If we all learn to get ourselves free, we won't need to spend years trying to find a church that offers deliverance help.

It is my goal in this Study Guide to give you enough knowledge to be able to get yourself and your family free of demons who influence your behavior negatively as well as break the Curse of Abuse off of your life forever.

GOD WANTS YOU TO BE FREE!

I was studying a book on spiritual warfare and making notes on a Saturday morning in 2012 and as I read the story of one lady's deliverance who had been bound with many spirits, I began to feel a terrible sadness rising upin my spirit and tears began rolling down my cheeks. I knew the Lord was sharing His sadness with me. Then He spoke to me:

I desire that My people would be free!

I never realized before that moment how terribly it grieves our Father's heart when we are bound up. It makes Him so sad when we are caught up in sin, when the enemy tempts and torments us. It makes Him sad when He provides us access to more than enough and we live in lack, unable to meet our own obligations, much less give into Kingdom work. It broke my heart to feel His grief and I just sat there weeping, thinking of how many thousands upon thousands of His people are bound right now, and who have no idea how to get free. Most would prefer to be free I think, but judging by the number of emails I get asking for help, I would say the majority can't find the help they need anywhere to get unbound.

In addition to you being in this battle, your children and loved ones also are. Children who grow up in an atmosphere of abuse often have defiled hearts as well as bodies. Their little hearts were broken – keepers of the issues of life shattered by the rage, cruelty, and violence they have witnessed, or worse, felt.

Their existence, bleak and unpredictable, holds little joy. A dysfunctional family does not teach you to speak what is in your heart because those around you do not understand themselves how to have healthy communication, and foster healthy relationships. When dealing with a volatile abuser, saying what you really think can get you hurt so you hold the pain inside and it festers under cover of anger. For years. Decades. A lifetime.

Children who grow up in an atmosphere of abuse will grow up to be abused or be abusive. There are few exceptions to this rule. Some will also grow up to abuse themselves.

HOSEA 4:6

6 MY PEOPLE ARE DESTROYED FOR LACK OF KNOWLEDGE: BECAUSE THOU HAST REJECTED KNOWLEDGE, I WILL ALSO REJECT THEE, THAT THOU SHALT BE NO PRIEST TO ME: SEEING THOU HAST FORGOTTEN THE LAW OF THY GOD, I WILL ALSO FORGET THY CHILDREN.

My people are destroyed for lack of knowledge.

There are many in the church who reject the knowledge about spiritual warfare and doing warfare, saying Jesus defeated the enemy and the battle is already won.

The battle IS already won. Jesus absolutely defeated the enemy, and we are not trying to add to His work, that isn't even possible. Spiritual warfare is not an insult to what Jesus did, it is simply standing up and *claiming* what He did. It is standing up and claiming what He gave you that the enemy has been trying to keep from you. It is refusing to be denied by the enemy what Jesus suffered to purchase for all of us.

We need both the authority that is ours through the victory Jesus won for us *and* the knowledge to use that authority. Authority without knowledge is useless.We must know how *and* when to use the authority that is ours through the precious Blood of Jesus.

Jesus cast out demons – a lot, when He walked on the earth.

But … you say Then Jesus went to the Cross. End of story, right? He defeated the devil so we're done, we can all sit down and rest in our freedom, right?

WRONG, but that IS exactly what the enemy WANTS you to think.

1 John 3:8

8 He that committeth sin is of the devil; for the devil sinneth from the beginning. For this purpose the Son of God was manifested, that he might destroy the works of the devil.

Colossians 2:15

15 And having spoiled principalities and powers, he made a shew of them openly, triumphing over them in it.

Ephesians Chapter 6 talks about taking the whole Armor of God – you don't need armor unless you're entering battle. These passages clearly define we're not fighting something flesh, we're fighting something spiritual. Period. Spiritual armor for spiritual warfare.

Ephesians 6:12-13

12 For we wrestle not against flesh and blood, but against principalities, against powers, against the rulers of the darkness of this world, against spiritual wickedness in high places.

13 Wherefore take unto you the whole armour of God, that ye may be able to withstand in the evil day, and having done all, to stand.

1. Spiritual warfare is not an _____ to what Jesus did, it is simply standing up and _____ what He did.

2. My people are destroyed for lack of _____.

3. Authority without knowledge is _____.

4. For this purpose the Son of God was manifested, that he might _____ the works of _____ _____.

5. And having spoiled _____ and _____, he made a shew of them openly, triumphing over them in it.

WE HAVE DOMINION

Jesus won the victory – He took back the right to the dominion Adam and Eve gave over to Satan in the Garden of Eden, the same authority to have dominion that was originally given to Adam by God Himself. When Adam and Eve chose to go Satan's way instead of God's, they lost that dominion.

Then precious Jesus came and was willing to bear all mankind's guilt for sin though He was not guilty of a single sin and to die an agonizing, hours long death on the Cross as the propitiation to purchase back that dominion. It belongs to Jesus, and He left us the weapons to administrate and enforce His victory and dominion, by commanding the enemy in His Name. But like in any battle, it is up to *us* to take up our weapons and fight the one who seeks to destroy us.

It's kind of like a contract, Jesus negotiated a new one for us. In fact, New Testament means New Covenant. A Covenant is actually stronger than a contract. The new one voids the terms of the old one and replaces it with new terms and stipulations.

But what happens if one of the parties to a contract is evil, ruthless and out to destroy? Do you just say, 'Oh, well, I have this new contract so I don't need to do anything??' The whole point of a written contract is so you can enforce your contractual rights, as often as is necessary.

And now we have a new contract signed in the precious Blood of the Son of God.

Jesus gave His disciples power to cast out demons. He also gave the 70 he sent out that power, so it clearly was not just for the 12 disciples. That means it's also for us. That means He still wants us using it.

EPHESIANS 6:12-13

12 FOR WE WRESTLE NOT AGAINST FLESH AND BLOOD, BUT AGAINST PRINCIPALITIES, AGAINST POWERS, AGAINST THE RULERS OF THE DARKNESS OF THIS WORLD, AGAINST SPIRITUAL WICKEDNESS IN HIGH PLACES.

13 WHEREFORE TAKE UNTO YOU THE WHOLE ARMOUR OF GOD, THAT YE MAY BE ABLE TO WITHSTAND IN THE EVIL DAY, AND HAVING DONE ALL, TO STAND.

Escaping Abuse Study Guide

1. It is up to *us* to take up our _____ and fight the one who seeks to destroy us.

2. Wherefore take unto you the whole _____ of God, that ye may be able to withstand in the evil day, and having done all, to stand.

3. New Testament means _____ _____.

4. Jesus' death on the Cross was the propitiation to purchase back _____.

5. How do we know the power to cast out demons was not just for the 12 disciples?

_____

_____

_____

_____

6. Write out your favorite verse about dominion.

_____

_____

_____

_____

DELIVERANCE DIDN'T END AT THE CROSS

Jesus showed us by sending out the 70 that the power and authority to take dominion over the demons was not just for the 12 disciples, we know that dominion is still for us today.

LUKE 10:1-2

1 AFTER THESE THINGS THE LORD APPOINTED OTHER SEVENTY ALSO, AND SENT THEM TWO AND TWO BEFORE HIS FACE INTO EVERY CITY AND PLACE, WHITHER HE HIMSELF WOULD COME.

2 THEREFORE SAID HE UNTO THEM, THE HARVEST TRULY IS GREAT, BUT THE LABOURERS ARE FEW: PRAY YE THEREFORE THE LORD OF THE HARVEST, THAT HE WOULD SEND FORTH LABOURERS INTO HIS HARVEST.

LUKE 10:17-20

17 AND THE SEVENTY RETURNED AGAIN WITH JOY, SAYING, LORD, EVEN THE DEVILS ARE SUBJECT UNTO US THROUGH THY NAME.

18 AND HE SAID UNTO THEM, I BEHELD SATAN AS LIGHTNING FALL FROM HEAVEN.

19 BEHOLD, I GIVE UNTO YOU POWER TO TREAD ON SERPENTS AND SCORPIONS, AND OVER ALL THE POWER OF THE ENEMY: AND NOTHING SHALL BY ANY MEANS HURT YOU.

20 NOTWITHSTANDING IN THIS REJOICE NOT, THAT THE SPIRITS ARE SUBJECT UNTO YOU; BUT RATHER REJOICE, BECAUSE YOUR NAMES ARE WRITTEN IN HEAVEN.

MARK 16:17-18

17 AND THESE SIGNS SHALL FOLLOW THEM THAT BELIEVE; IN MY NAME SHALL THEY CAST OUT DEVILS; THEY SHALL SPEAK WITH NEW TONGUES;

18 THEY SHALL TAKE UP SERPENTS; AND IF THEY DRINK ANY DEADLY THING, IT SHALL NOT HURT THEM; THEY SHALL LAY HANDS ON THE SICK, AND THEY SHALL RECOVER.

Many Christians don't want to get involved in spiritual warfare because they fear retaliation from the devil and his demons. The devil wants nothing more than these two things – for you to not believe he is real, thinking he is just a cartoon character someone made up, or for you to fear him, reverencing his power more than the power of Jesus (a form of worship of the devil), keeping you from fighting him at all. Meanwhile, he'll go on wreaking havoc in your life, and in the lives of those you love.

Make no mistake – the enemy is a liar, a murderer, and a destroyer. And he hates you.

The devil is after your faith, your mind, your will, your emotions, your body, your health, your sanity, your children, your spouse, your family, your marriage, your business, your freedom, your finances, your future, your calling, and anything else good or Godly you have.

Demons are a lot like snakes. I grew up fearing snakes until I found out they are far more afraid of me than I am of them. There are a couple of exceptions to that rule, of course – one is cottonmouths.

Cottonmouth snakes, also known as water moccasins, aren't afraid of anything. When I worked in the swamps of Louisiana in the 90s with an Oil and Gas Exploration crew, we all knew to watch out for them. They are so aggressive, they will strike at a passing airboat.

But demons are another story. Demons like to make you afraid, and they know what you are afraid of. The good news is, if you believe Jesus died on the Cross for your sins and God raised Him from the dead, then you have power and authority over demons. They have to obey the commands you give them in the Name of Jesus. If you tell them to be cast out, they must depart.

Be aware, if you cast a demon out of a person in Jesus Name, it must leave the person, but it can still stay in the room. But if you cast a demon out **and command it to go to the Abyss in Jesus**

Name, then it must go into the Abyss. That is the reason I always command them to go into the Abyss, and to take their filth and their seeds with them.

If you don't think demons have seeds, read this verse in Genesis, where the Lord God was cursing the devil:

GENESIS 3:15

15 AND I WILL PUT ENMITY BETWEEN THEE AND THE WOMAN, AND BETWEEN THY SEED AND HER SEED; IT SHALL BRUISE THY HEAD, AND THOU SHALT BRUISE HIS HEEL. (EMPHASIS MINE)

So it is also important to command the demonic seeds out with the demons, in Jesus Name.

If you bind demons up, they are bound.

I have heard many Christians pray prayers for God to deliver them of this or that, but He left *us* the weapons to enforce the deliverance that is already ours, that Satan is trying to bully us out of. We are not beggars, we are believers, and you will gain a great sense of empowerment when you experience commanding demons and getting free of their destructive work in your life.

Many Christians do not believe a demon can attach to a Christian. Can they? You bet. We have biblical examples that show that. Acts 5:3 is the one I think shows it best.

ACTS 5:3

3 BUT PETER SAID, ANANIAS, WHY HATH SATAN FILLED THINE HEART TO LIE TO THE HOLY GHOST, AND TO KEEP BACK PART OF THE PRICE OF THE LAND?

Acts 5:3 shows us that Christians can indeed have a demon. Satan filled Ananias' heart with a lying demon, and Ananias was a Christian.

Escaping Abuse Study Guide

1. Behold, I give unto you _____ to tread on serpents and scorpions, and over all the _____ of the enemy: and nothing shall by any means _____ you.

2. Notwithstanding in this _____ not, that the spirits are subject unto you; but rather _____, because your names are written in heaven.

3. And these signs shall follow them that believe; In my name shall they _____ _____ _____; they shall speak with _____ _____;

4. The enemy is a _____, a _____, and a _____.

5. Demons are a lot like _____.

6. If you tell demons to be cast out, they must _____.

   It is important to command the demonic _____ out with the demons.

7. If you bind demons up, they are _____.

8. Acts 5:3 shows us that Christians can indeed have a _____.

ARE WE DELIVERED OF DEMONS AS SOON AS WE GET SAVED?

Many Christians believe when we get saved, we automatically get delivered of every demon. I can personally testify this was not the case with me, or with anyone I have ever met. I have not been able to find any scripture in the Bible that says we are delivered of every demon the minute we get saved. If we did, there would be *far* less sin in the church than we are seeing. If there are no demons in Christians, then why do we see pastors and other leaders falling into every conceivable type of sin?

Is it just their flesh? Some of it. Not every sin is because there's a demon whispering in your ear. Sometimes, it is simply the appetites of our flesh that have not been crucified yet. Often, we are our own worst enemies. In that split second when we are faced with doing what's right or doing what's wrong, we choose to do what's wrong.

So if it's not always the appetites of the flesh, that only leaves one other influence – the influence of the Evil One, Satan.

I don't believe a Christian can be possessed, but it is debatable, possession being total demonic control. But either way, we can definitely be oppressed – influenced and afflicted, by demonic forces.

If we are saved, our sins have been washed away by the Blood of Jesus. The demons are still there, though, and so are the appetites of our flesh, and all our bad habits. Another thing that is there, especially in victims of abuse, are soul wounds, and demons access us and torment us through those unhealed wounds. And soul wounds stay open and fester until we forgive those who hurt us.

The bottom line is this – you can leave the enemy alone if you want to, but don't expect him to leave you – or your loved ones – alone. Now or ever. The only humans he leaves alone are those who are already working for him. He's been watching you and working on you since you were in the womb, and he's not about to stop now.

Will he retaliate? He might try, but who has the real power here? If you have all the power over him, who is in charge if he *does* retaliate? You are.

LUKE 10:19

19 BEHOLD, I GIVE UNTO YOU POWER TO TREAD ON SERPENTS AND SCORPIONS, AND OVER ALL THE POWER OF THE ENEMY: AND NOTHING SHALL BY ANY MEANS HURT YOU.

An interesting note about Luke 10:19 is that sexual perversion spirits are often seen as frogs, serpents and scorpions.

It's time to armor up and learn to fight. It's time to clean up the sin in our lives by making the right choice each time temptation calls, and send the enemy packing. It's time to take back our minds, our families, our marriages, our health and our finances. It's time to stop taking the enemy's flack and show him Whose child you are.

Escaping Abuse Study Guide

1. Some of it. Not every _____ is because there's a demon whispering in your ear. Sometimes, it is simply the _____ of our flesh that have not been crucified yet.

2. We can definitely be oppressed – influenced and afflicted, by _____ forces.

3. If we are saved, our _____ have been washed away by the Blood of Jesus. The demons are still there, though, and so are the _____ of our flesh, and all our _____ _____.

4. Behold, I give unto you _____ to tread on serpents and scorpions, and over all the _____ of the enemy: and nothing shall by any means hurt you.

5. Write out your favorite verse about our power over demons

_____

_____

_____

_____

_____

_____

HOW DEMONS GAIN ACCESS TO YOU

DEMONS ACCESS US THROUGH PEOPLE

There are many ways demons can gain access to humans, beginning with the iniquity of our forefathers – our generational bloodline for up to four generations back (up to ten where the Curse of Illegitimacy is concerned – for those conceived out of wedlock), though probably the most common way they gain access is by us letting them in through sinful thoughts and actions; they can also access us through soul ties, soul wounds, unholy associations and cursed objects around us. They can access us through occult related activities like reading horoscopes, going to psychic readers, tarot cards, Ouija boards, and more.

Our fight against demons must always begin with us, and our homes. We must examine ourselves for harsh thoughts and actions towards others, sinful desires we have refused to surrender, for unholy activities and associations we know do not belong in the lives of devoted Christians, but which we have ignored God's promptings about.

No amount of spiritual warfare or casting out of demons will keep us free if there is sin in our own camp.

Our second area of attack should be to check the level to which our mind has been renewed in the Word of God. Our minds are our control centers for our behavior. We must all spend time in the Word of God every day because if we don't know the truth, we won't recognize deception when Satan whispers it to us.

WAYS DEMONS ACCESS US THROUGH OTHER PEOPLE

- Generational iniquities on our bloodline such as abuse, perversion and poverty are direct inroads for demons to access us

- Soul Ties are formed any time there is an intimate connection, whether physical or emotional, including all forms of sex and pornography. We also form soul ties in friendship.

- Sometimes demonic spirits transfer when a loved one dies – the spirits that were on them are looking for a new live host. The Spirit of Suicide is especially dangerous in this way, because it can cause a 'chain reaction' of suicides by moving from family member to family member or within a city or school. This demon attempted to do this in my own family.

- Demons like anger, rage, violence and rape can access us through another person who commits these acts against us.

- Being angry and getting offended lets demons in. Rejection by another person also lets in a demon. (Spirit of Anger, Spirit of Offense, Spirit of Rejection)

- Word Curses – These often happen during childhood. This is a big one and these fiery darts wound our spirits.

Escaping Abuse Study Guide

1. Probably the most common way demons gain access is by us letting them in through _____ _____ and _____.

2. Our fight against demons must always begin with _____, and our _____.

3. No amount of spiritual warfare or casting out of demons will keep us free if there is _____ in our own camp.

4. Our second area of attack should be to check the level to which our _____ has been _____ in the Word of God.

5. Can you recall a story where someone you knew was accessed by a demon? What happened?

_____

_____

_____

_____

_____

_____

DEMONS ACCESS US THROUGH PLACES AND OBJECTS

TERRITORIES RULED BY PRINCIPALITIES

Every territory – every nation, state, city, regional area and even neighborhood has a principality demon (at least one) ruling over it. Whenever we move into an area, those territorial spirits such as Poverty, Pride, Perversion and others have access to us, too.

Demons can access us if we enter a sinful place, such as a bar or strip club, or House of Voodoo, etc. When you enter a place like that, you are in the Devil's territory and he has a right to afflict you. You cannot, unless the Lord directly commanded you to enter a sinful place, expect immunity from those demonic influences.

DEMONS ACCESS US THROUGH OBJECTS

The Bible declares certain objects to be cursed objects. If you want to get free of demonic influence, these are objects you must get rid of and have no association with them at all. They are open doors to demons to enter your life, your home and your family.

OBJECTS TO REMOVE FROM YOUR LIFE

- Any picture that has an evil or demonic look to it – this includes skulls. If it looks or represents something evil or fearful looking, it is demonic. No exceptions! Skulls and zombies both represent death and evil.

- Demons can access us if we enter a sinful place, such as a bar or strip club, or House of Voodoo. Years ago a friend sent me a photo that the Lord revealed had a Spirit of Lust attached to it. The Lord instructed me to burn the photo and cast the spirit out of me and out of my house, which I did. He revealed to me this spirit is working through fashion magazines and affecting millions of young women, causing them to want to look and be seductive. This spirit is not fashionable, it is demonic.

- Pornography – always has lust and seduction, perversion and masturbation spirits attached to it. It may also have other spirits as well.

- Demonic or horror movies – always have the Spirit of Fear attached, among others. These spirits enter your home when you view the movie.

- Wicked album and CD covers – demonic or wicked looking images on covers always carry demons. I once knew a worship leader who sensed something evil had moved into his home, where his son had previously resided. He asked me for help discerning it. The Lord would not allow me to enter the room, but showed me a CD cover with a wicked looking demonic image on it. I told the man what the Lord said. He began rifling through stuff left behind by his son, and sure enough, there was a cover. Once removed from the home, he was able to cast out the spirit and have peace again.

- Anything related to astrology (this includes jewelry).

- Ouija boards – extremely evil. I consider these gateways to hell.

- Another Unrelated Area to Watch Out for is FurntiurePurchased Second Hand – Once I was walking through the basement of an old church building with some friends, and as we passed on opposite sides of an old hospital bed, I saw a Spirit of Death was attached to it. My friends saw it at the same time and commanded it to be cast out. In my spirit, I saw that an elderly man had died in the bed, and the Spirit of Death stayed behind to wait for the next live host to attach to.

JOSHUA 7:1

7 BUT THE CHILDREN OF ISRAEL COMMITTED A TRESPASS IN THE ACCURSED THING: FOR ACHAN, THE SON OF CARMI, THE SON OF ZABDI, THE SON OF ZERAH, OF THE TRIBE OF JUDAH, TOOK OF THE ACCURSED THING: AND THE ANGER OF THE LORD WAS KINDLED AGAINST THE CHILDREN OF ISRAEL.

JOSHUA 22:20

20 DID NOT ACHAN THE SON OF ZERAH COMMIT A TRESPASS IN THE ACCURSED THING, AND WRATH FELL ON ALL THE CONGREGATION OF ISRAEL? AND THAT MAN PERISHED NOT ALONE IN HIS INIQUITY.

Escaping Abuse Study Guide

1. Every _____ – every nation, state, city, regional area and even neighborhood has at least one principality demon ruling over it.

2. _____ can access us if we enter a sinful place, such as a bar or strip club, or House of Voodoo.

3. The Bible declares certain objects to be _____ objects.

4. Demonic or horror _____ – always have the Spirit of Fear attached, among others.

5. Demonic or wicked looking _____ on covers always carry demons.

6. After doing this lesson, what items in your house need to be removed?

_____

_____

_____

_____

SPECIAL CATEGORIES OF OBJECTS

There are two areas of cursed objects I want to put special emphasis on that I have seen bring fast and serious consequences – these objects should be removed immediately from your home and, if possible, burned..These are very, very serious.

- Anything occult, witchcraft, or 'New Age' related. These categories include, but are not limited to: Tarot Cards, crystals, zodiac or horoscope related items, anything related to psychic abilities or readings, spell casting, charms, chanting, Ouija boards, mediums, chakras, astral projection, reiki, levitation, remote viewing, Feng Shui, Voodoo, witchcraft, conjuring spirits, clairvoyance, mysticism, candle gazing and more.

- Absolutely anything related to another religion – **not even as art** – I cannot stress this enough.

I have seen statues of Buddha being called art in the homes of Christians before who insist it isn't a problem. You may as well have a statue of Satan in your home as to have a statue of a false god or goddess.

Buddha is not art to the Lord, he is a false god that Satan hides behind. He sees that 'art' as another god where only He should be allowed. Even pictures of these will bring a curse into your home, where it will have access to everyone there. The same goes for businesses.

I once walked into the business of a new friend and, as we were talking, I saw a small figurine of Buddha on a shelf. I felt strongly the statue was going to bring destruction to his business, since he was a Christian, and I told him as much.

He claimed it was just art. I reiterated what the Lord had shown me. A few days later, he claimed to have gotten rid of it. I felt the Lord showed me he had only moved it.

A month later, his business closed. It never reopened.

Escaping Abuse Study Guide

1. Anything _____, witchcraft, or 'New Age' related should be removed from your home.

2. Anything related to another _____ should be immediately removed from your home.

3. You may as well have a statue of _____ in your home as to have a statue of a false god or goddess like Buddha.

4. Buddha is not art to the Lord, he is a false god that_____ hides behind.

5. Write out your favorite verse about cursed objects.

_____

_____

_____

_____

_____

_____

_____

WAYS DEMONS AFFLICT YOU

In order to understand why we need to get rid of demons and curses, we need to understand something about the damage and destruction they do.

- Demons attack your mind, emotions and will. These three things make up your soul man. They distract you, bring depression, addictive thought patterns, and more. Depression is always a demon.

- Whenever I see someone's mind afflicted, I always look for something linked to witchcraft. Witchcraft (including drugs) and witchcraft related items always bring problems related to the mind.

- Demons attack your body – lethargy, sickness of all kinds (including cancer), sudden pains, and feelings of choking.

- Demons leave wounds on your spirit through the words and actions of others. These are called soul wounds. Prolonged abuse brings many soul wounds, all related to fear. Soul wounds are doorways to demons who torment you until you are able to forgive the person who wounded you.

- Demons work inwardly as well as outwardly. They work inwardly towards you to abuse yourself – with suicidal thoughts, with addictions, self-mutilation, and eating disorders.

- Demons work in concert with one another to increase their destruction. Rejection and Offense are examples of demons who work in pairs.

- Demons influence us to commit sins. Some demonic forces are so strong you feel driven to do certain sins again and again, and you don't understand why you do them. The devil will be sure to bring shame, regret and remorse afterwards, too.

Maybe you think after committing a sin yet again "What's wrong with me?" The good news is, it *isn't* just you – there's another influence at work. But you must fight it, or will eventually take over it.

1. Demons _____ your mind, emotions and will, which make up your soul.

2. _____ and related items always bring problems related to the mind.

3. Demons leave _____ on your spirit through the words and actions of others. These are called _____ _____.

4. Soul wounds are _____ to demons who torment you until you are able to _____ the person who wounded you.

5. Demons work _____ as well as outwardly.

6. Demons work in _____with one another to increase their destruction.

7. Demons _____ us to commit sins.

AUTHORITY TO CAST OUT DEMONS

Remember, you have no authority to cast out a demon unless you are saved – unless you have given your life to Jesus.

There is a story in Acts Chapter 19, about some men who tried to cast out a demon who were not saved and what happened to them. They were called the Sons of Sceva.

Acts 19:11-16

11 And God wrought special miracles by the hands of Paul:

12 So that from his body were brought unto the sick handkerchiefs or aprons, and the diseases departed from them, and the evil spirits went out of them.

13 Then certain of the vagabond Jews, exorcists, took upon them to call over them which had evil spirits the name of the Lord Jesus, saying, We adjure you by Jesus whom Paul preacheth.

14 And there were seven sons of one Sceva, a Jew, and chief of the priests, which did so.

15 And the evil spirit answered and said, Jesus I know, and Paul I know; but who are ye?

16 And the man in whom the evil spirit was leaped on them, and overcame them, and prevailed against them, so that they fled out of that house naked and wounded.

Escaping Abuse Study Guide

1. You have no authority to cast out a demon unless you are
_____.

2. And the man in whom the _____ _____was
leaped on them, and overcame them, and prevailed against them,
so that they fled out of that house naked and wounded.

3. Write out your favorite verse about authority over demons

_____

_____

_____

_____

_____

HOW TO STOP DEMONS FROM COMING THROUGH SOUL TUNNELS

Any time you are having cravings or urges that are abnormal for you, it is important to investigate the subject of Soul Ties, or Soul Tunnels as I like to call them.

Any time you become acquainted or intimate with another person in any way, even by just fantasizing about them, you open up a soul tunnel where demons attached to them can access you. In order to get free of these tunnels, we must break the soul ties and cast out the demons that came in with them.

1. **OBJECTS**. You must get rid of all objects related to the soul tie. In romantic relationships, this could be love letters, photographs of that person or the two of you together, gifts from them including jewelry, rings that symbolized the relationship.

Many people have asked me about breaking soul ties with a spouse. I can only say from personal experience that I was never able to break the soul tie with my first husband. That marriage was God-ordained though it was abusive, and I found I had no power over the soul ties, even years after we divorced. This may be because we had children together, I am not sure. Marriages after the first one, if not God ordained, I think you can break soul ties with.

2. **FANTASIES**. Renounce all fantasies about that person, whether relationship based or sexual in nature. Matthew 5:28 confirms for us that sexual fantasies create soul ties just like having physical intimacy does.

MATTHEW 5:28

28 BUT I SAY UNTO YOU, THAT WHOSOEVER LOOKETH ON A WOMAN TO LUST AFTER HER HATH COMMITTED ADULTERY WITH HER ALREADY IN HIS HEART.

The heart is where the affections lie and affections keep soul ties alive. If looking causes adultery, then it also causes fornication, and many other sins, depending on what you were fantasizing. Fantasies allow demons access to you, and cause soul ties to be formed. If fantasies let demons in, then we need to renounce the fantasies and ask forgiveness so we can cast the demons back out.

3. **SPOKEN COVENANTS.** Renounce any covenants you made with that person – vows, commitments – if you said you would be with them forever, that you were their partner forever, that you would never leave them, that you would never love another person – whatever you said, you need to renounce those spoken covenants to remove the soul tie in the spiritual realm. In addition, spoken covenants can actually cause the thing that was spoken to come to pass.

4. **FORGIVE AND RELEASE ANY BITTERNESS**.

Search your heart for any unforgiveness you might have towards the person or any anger or bitterness about the relationship. Unforgiveness gives the demons the right to stay and hang out with you, so we need to deal with that or your freedom will just be wishful thinking.

5. **REPENT OF AND RENOUNCE THE RELATIONSHIP ITSELF IF IT WAS UNGODLY, AND ASK FORGIVENESS**.

If the relationship itself was ungodly, you need to ask forgiveness for your involvement in it. (one example of an ungodly relationship would be an adulterous one) You also need to renounce it and turn away from it. Renouncing something or someone releases you from it spiritually in a very important way.

You must be willing to completely cut every tie and all contact with the person in order to break the soul tie. Otherwise, the soul tie stays active.

Escaping Abuse Study Guide

1. Any time you are having cravings or urges that are abnormal for you, it is important to investigate the subject of _____ _____.

2. _____ _____ confirms for us that fantasies create soul ties just as physical intimacy does.

3. But I say unto you, That whosoever _____ on a woman to lust after her hath committed adultery with her already in his heart.

4. The heart is where the _____ lie and _____ keep soul ties alive.

5. _____ _____ can actually cause the thing that was spoken to come to pass.

6. _____ gives the demons the right to stay.

7. Any time you are having cravings or urges that are abnormal for you, it is important to investigate the subject of _____ _____, or _____ _____.

8. Any time you become acquainted or intimate with another person in any way, even by just fantasizing about them, you open up a _____ _____where demons attached to them can _____ you.

9. Write out how you are cutting off all contact from your abusive relationship

_____

_____

_____

_____

_____

PRAYER TO BREAK THE SOUL TIE

Say this prayer out loud to break the soul tie in your abusive relationship.

Lord, in the mighty and matchless Name of Jesus Christ, I renounce and break and I ask You to completely sever the soul tie between me and _____. I praise You, Lord, that I know as I pray this, it is being done, and You are completely separating my soul from _____'s soul in the spiritual realm. Amen.

BIND UP RETALIATION

Pray to bind up any demonic retaliation in the Name of Jesus now by saying the following prayer out loud. Satan is losing ground in your life as you are breaking soul ties and taking the necessary steps to get free, and he doesn't like it.

In the Name of Jesus, I bind up any demonic retaliation that could or would come, and I forbid any assignments of retaliation against me or anyone around me for breaking this soul tie. Thank You, Lord. I know You are well able to protect me and all those I love. Amen.

THE POWER OF YOUR WORDS

Our words have the power to produce. Every word you speak either produces more life, or it produces more death. We are made in God's image, and He spoke the whole universe into existence.

It is of the utmost importance that we only speak words of life over those we love. Otherwise, we are speaking word curses and our words can cause the things we speak to come to pass, because of the great power behind our words.

Do you often speak of your spouse and children in positive and flattering ways? Or do you sit around talking about how you think your wife or husband is cheating on you? Do you call them names? Do you call them wicked, ugly, and unfaithful?

Do you speak life, calling them good looking, faithful, and prosperous? Do you want him or her to be a person of God? Then call them a person of God. Do you want them to be faithful and true? Then call them faithful and true each time you speak about him or her. Call him or her strong and righteous. Call your children obedient and responsible, even if you do not see those traits in them. *Especially* if you don't see those traits in them. Your words can help or hinder these things coming to pass.

Always speak what you want, not what you have.

FORGIVENESS BRINGS HEALING

One of the very difficult aspects of being an abuse survivor is the command to forgive. Years of abuse and the painful memories and damage it leaves make forgiving a true challenge.

In 1997, I had been in my walk with the Lord for about a year when, reading my Bible one night, I came across Matthew 6:14-15.

MATTHEW 6:14-15

14 FOR IF YE FORGIVE MEN THEIR TRESPASSES, YOUR HEAVENLY FATHER WILL ALSO FORGIVE YOU:

15 BUT IF YE FORGIVE NOT MEN THEIR TRESPASSES, NEITHER WILL YOUR FATHER FORGIVE YOUR TRESPASSES.

When I read that I would not be forgiven if I did not forgive everyone else, I panicked. I was not willing to go to hell for anyone, no matter what they had done to me. I quickly made a list of everyone I felt I had unforgiveness towards, including my ex-husband.

I then got down on my knees and went down the list, confessing to the Lord my unforgiveness and asking for forgiveness, as well as help forgiving, and doing my best to release every instance to the Lord. I saved my ex-husband for last. I knew almost 12 years of abuse would be the hardest to forgive.

As I prayed to forgive him, I felt I could not do it. I did not see how I could let go of all that pain and anger. I knew that meant I would go to hell when I died. I became really afraid then. What if I left my apartment the next day and got killed in a car accident? There would be no more chances to repent and forgive!

Lord, please help me! I don't know how to forgive Rick for all those miserable years and I am not willing to go to hell over that. I am not getting up off this floor until You help me forgive him – I can't take the chance I could die suddenly and have unforgiveness!

I continued crying out to the Lord, and about five minutes later I felt a touch from heaven. Suddenly my spirit was flooded with visions of many terrible things my ex-husband had suffered as a child, and the Lord filled my soul with compassion for him. For the first time since our divorce, I was genuinely able to pray for him to be saved and blessed, and I continued to do that from that night forward until his death in 2010.

Almost every memory of the abuse left me in that moment when the Lord touched me, and they have never returned. What little I could still remember had no emotion connected to it, a huge change from before. All the anger, all the pain, all the fear, was completely gone. The torment of all those years was finally over.

Forgiving the man who had abused me for almost 12 very long years had set *me* free.

When you are able to forgive your abuser, you will be set free, too.

Escaping Abuse Study Guide

1. One of the very difficult aspects of being an abuse survivor is the command to forgive.

2. BUT IF YE FORGIVE NOT MEN THEIR TRESPASSES, NEITHER WILL YOUR FATHER FORGIVE YOUR TRESPASSES.

3. When you are able to forgive your abuser, you will be set free, too.

4. Have you ever tried to forgive the person who abused you?
_____

Did you succeed?
_____

What happened?
_____

_____

_____

_____

_____

_____

_____

_____

_____

WHAT MAKES YOU AN ABUSE MAGNET – A LITTLE KNOWN SPIRITUAL LAW ABOUT DEMONS

It is helpful when working to remove a curse from your life to understand some things about the nature of the demonic forces you are dealing with.

First, demonic forces are pure evil, there is no good in them and there is never any good intent in them towards you. Demons hate humans with a passion. I once felt a demon's hatred towards me, and it was beyond intense. Demons constantly work to deceive humans with any lie they can sell us. Their job is to act out their natures through us and cause sin. Period.

Demons long to express their nature through you. If it is a Demon of Lust, it has no body but it has lust, so it wants to express its lust using *your* body. If it is a Demon of Violence, it wants to commit violence using *your* body. A Demon of Anger wants to express its anger through you towards those around you. And on and on. Lust, violence and anger are certainly not the fruits of God's Spirit, are they?

I learned something new and very important about demons when I was shown the vision of how the Curse of Abuse manifested in my family of origin.

I had known for years that a demon attached to someone could act outwardly, or inwardly. A good example of this is the Spirit of Murder. A Spirit of Murder on someone may cause them to murder another person and then it may turn inward against its host, and persuade the host to murder his or her self (suicide). Whenever you see a murder-suicide in the news, this is what you are seeing.

When I was shown the vision, I learned that demons not only act outwardly through you to sin, they draw to you whatever sin they represent as well. I was shown that this was the reason sexual abuse happened to me in early childhood, and by more than one abuser. The Curse of Abuse was present, acting as the open door. I was not old enough for the Spirit of Abuse to act out towards others through me really, so it drew abusers to me and caused the abuse that way. I was shocked to learn demons could draw sin to me like that.

The bottom line is this: Demons have a job to cause a particular sin. It does not matter to them if they cause you to do the sin or someone else to do the sin against you, as long as the sin happens.

So I prayed about it.

Okay, Lord, if this is true, then it must be reflected some place in scripture. Please show me where. (I knew it was true since He had shown it to me, but I also know that scripture will confirm any spiritual law).

He answered me.

Cain.

I grabbed my Bible and began looking for the reference. Genesis. Cain. There it was!

GENESIS 4:14

14 BEHOLD, THOU HAST DRIVEN ME OUT THIS DAY FROM THE FACE OF THE EARTH; AND FROM THY FACE SHALL I BE HID; AND I SHALL BE A FUGITIVE AND A VAGABOND IN THE EARTH; AND IT SHALL COME TO PASS, THAT EVERY ONE THAT FINDETH ME SHALL SLAY ME.

Every one that findeth me shall slay me... They would slay him because the Spirit of Murder that had acted through him to kill Abel would now draw murder to *him*!

So demons not only function outwardly towards others, and inwardly towards their host, but they also function like magnets – drawing others with the same type of demons on them to the host to cause the sin to be committed against them. Which means anyone who has a Curse of Abuse on them is literally a magnet for abusers of every type, for as long as they live unless they break the Curse of Abuse and cast out those spirits. Because a curse continues until someone has the knowledge to remove it.

It is also important to note that if the Curse of Abuse is on the Father or Grandfathers, it is always on the children as well. It may manifest in various ways. They will be abusers, victims, and they may even alternate between the two, but the curse continues until it is broken properly.

I sat in shock that morning on my bed and watched the vision in my spirit as the Lord showed me each person in my family and how the Curse of Abuse had affected their life. In some, it drew them to mates who abused them physically, verbally, sexually, or a combination. In others, they became the abusers.

Escaping Abuse Study Guide

1. _____ constantly work to deceive humans with any lie they can sell us. Their job is to act out their natures through us and cause sin.

2. Demons long to express their _____ through you.

3. Demons not only act outwardly through you to sin, they draw to you whatever _____ they represent as well.

4. *Every one that findeth me shall slay me*... They would slay him because the Spirit of Murder that had acted through him to kill Abel would now _____ murder to *him.*

5. Anyone who has a Curse of Abuse on them is literally a _____ for abusers of every type.

6. If the Curse of Abuse is on the Father, or Grandfathers, it is _____ on the children as well.

7. Do you think the Curse of Abuse is on you?

_____

Explain why.

_____

_____

_____

_____

PRAYER TO BREAK THE CURSE OF ABUSE

So in dealing with the Curse of Abuse, we want to first remove the demons' right to be there by breaking the curse and then cast out the demons, commanding them to go into the Abyss, so they can't come back, in order to completely stop their destruction. It must be noted that you cannot break the curse off someone else's life (other than a very small child who is still completely under your care and control). Each person needs to break it off themselves.

Lord God in heaven, I submit myself to You. I ask for Your help is this process of deliverance, and in ridding myself of abuse forever. I know I have authority over ALL the power of the enemy according to Luke 10:19. I believe Jesus is truly Your resurrected Son who died for my sins, who left me this authority.

I come before You now and repent on behalf of my forefathers for the sin of abuse, and I ask You to remove the iniquity of abuse from my life, that I may more fully serve You, Lord. I also repent and ask for forgiveness of any sins of abuse I have ever committed, knowingly or unknowingly, and I receive Your forgiveness now.

And now, in the mighty and matchless Name of My Lord and Savior Jesus Christ of Nazareth, I declare the Curse of Abuse to be broken off my life! I command the Curse of Abuse to fall to the ground and become as nothing in Jesus mighty Name.

I command you, Spirit of Abuse, to clean up your filth, pick up your seeds and go immediately in the the Abyss, in Jesus Name. Go NOW!

(Repeat the last paragraph for each demon you think may be there, substituting that spirits name in the place of abuse). You must command them to leave one by one, in Jesus Name, or they will not leave.

I always praise God when I am done for His authority and the shed blood of Jesus to cast out demons and break curses.

DEMON HIT LIST FOR THE CURSE OF ABUSE

Think of a house with the door standing open. Okay, the house is your body, your life. The Curse of Abuse is the open door to that house. In order to get that house completely cleaned out, we need to identify and evict as many of the demons the curse has let in as possible.

The demons associated with the Curse of Abuse on each person will be different, but following is a hit list to begin with of the most common ones. By the time I had broken the Curse of Abuse off myself and cast out every demon I thought might be there, I had covered more than fifty. But those may not be the same demons you have.

Two of the ways to determine which demons you are dealing with are:

1. Let the Holy Spirit reveal them to you.

2. Name them according to the sins they cause.

Both of these methods work.

DEMON HIT LIST
- Abuse
- Violence
- Hate
- Murder/Suicide
- Rape
- Rejection
- Divorce and Division

- Spirits of Sexual Perversion

- Lawlessness and Rebellion

- Humiliation

- Take it (a demon that influences you to just take abuse from anyone)

Knowledge without application is just words on a page. You must do the steps of breaking the curse and casting out the demons one-by-one if you want to be free of the Curse of Abuse and all the demons it has let into your life.

POST TRAUMATIC STRESS DISORDER – HOW TO GET FREE

Many abuse victims suffer from the horrific effects of Post Traumatic Stress Disorder, also known as PTSD. The medical community has no cure for PTSD, but God does have a cure.

I was diagnosed with PTSD in the early 1990s. I had horrific, terrifying flashbacks and nightmare cycles that would last as long as ten days at a stretch. The flashbacks I suffered from seemed to go back to a particularly bad night of abuse in the mid 80s that happened in McKinney, Texas.

Months after the Lord helped me to forgive my ex-husband in 1997, I was living in Sayre, Oklahoma waiting for the Lord to direct my next move. One of the ladies I sang with at church came to my house one morning and casually said, "Hey, I was praying for you this morning and the Lord told me to tell you He has healed all the emotional effects of your marriage."

My friend Beverly B., who brought me the message, did not know I had been diagnosed with PTSD in the early 1990s, and that I had suffered many years of nightmares and full-blown flashbacks of the abuse since leaving my ex-husband in 1987.

It was all I could do not to jump up and go into my Happy Dance. He had set me free from those awful nightmares and flashbacks. Free! He had sent His Word and healed me!

WHAT IS PTSD?

The definition given by the National Center for PTSD is:

PTSD (posttraumatic stress disorder) is a mental health problem that some people develop after experiencing or witnessing a life-threatening event, like combat, a natural disaster, a car accident, or sexual assault.

After much prayer following my forgiveness experience with the Lord, I came to understand that it was forgiving my ex-husband that healed me of PTSD.

In refusing to forgive someone, we set in motion a spiritual law and we are then turned over to the tormentors. PTSD is the result.

PARABLE OF THE UNFORGIVING SERVANT

In Matthew Chapter 18, we can see that the unforgiving servant was turned over to the tormentors for not forgiving.

Parable of the Unforgiving Servant

MATTHEW 18:23-35

23 THEREFORE IS THE KINGDOM OF HEAVEN LIKENED UNTO A CERTAIN KING, WHICH WOULD TAKE ACCOUNT OF HIS SERVANTS.

24 AND WHEN HE HAD BEGUN TO RECKON, ONE WAS BROUGHT UNTO HIM, WHICH OWED HIM TEN THOUSAND TALENTS.

25 BUT FORASMUCH AS HE HAD NOT TO PAY, HIS LORD COMMANDED HIM TO BE SOLD, AND HIS WIFE, AND CHILDREN, AND ALL THAT HE HAD, AND PAYMENT TO BE MADE.

26 THE SERVANT THEREFORE FELL DOWN, AND WORSHIPPED HIM, SAYING, LORD, HAVE PATIENCE WITH ME, AND I WILL PAY THEE ALL.

27 THEN THE LORD OF THAT SERVANT WAS MOVED WITH COMPASSION, AND LOOSED HIM, AND FORGAVE HIM THE DEBT.

28 BUT THE SAME SERVANT WENT OUT, AND FOUND ONE OF HIS FELLOWSERVANTS, WHICH OWED HIM AN HUNDRED PENCE: AND HE LAID HANDS ON HIM, AND TOOK HIM BY THE THROAT, SAYING, PAY ME THAT THOU OWEST.

29 AND HIS FELLOWSERVANT FELL DOWN AT HIS FEET, AND BESOUGHT HIM, SAYING, HAVE PATIENCE WITH ME, AND I WILL PAY THEE ALL.

30 AND HE WOULD NOT: BUT WENT AND CAST HIM INTO PRISON, TILL HE SHOULD PAY THE DEBT.

31 SO WHEN HIS FELLOWSERVANTS SAW WHAT WAS DONE, THEY WERE VERY SORRY, AND CAME AND TOLD UNTO THEIR LORD ALL THAT WAS DONE.

32 THEN HIS LORD, AFTER THAT HE HAD CALLED HIM, SAID UNTO HIM, O THOU WICKED SERVANT, I FORGAVE THEE ALL THAT DEBT, BECAUSE THOU DESIREDST ME:

33 SHOULDEST NOT THOU ALSO HAVE HAD COMPASSION ON THY FELLOWSERVANT, EVEN AS I HAD PITY ON THEE?

34 AND HIS LORD WAS WROTH, AND DELIVERED HIM TO THE TORMENTORS, TILL HE SHOULD PAY ALL THAT WAS DUE UNTO HIM.

VERSE 35 TELLS US THE SAME THING WILL HAPPEN TO US IF *WE* DO NOT FORGIVE:

35 SO LIKEWISE SHALL MY HEAVENLY FATHER DO ALSO UNTO YOU, IF YE FROM YOUR HEARTS FORGIVE NOT EVERY ONE HIS BROTHER THEIR TRESPASSES.

If unforgiveness brings the tormentors, it makes perfect sense that forgiving would send them away again. Forgiveness brings complete healing from PTSD.

WAR AND PTSD

Some warriors who have been forced to do terrible things in war, come back almost unable to function because of Post Traumatic Stress Disorder. Sometimes in these cases, the person they need to forgive is themselves. Sometimes it may even be the President who sent them to war, or a commanding officer.

Bitterness and resentment also lead to unforgiveness. No trauma, no wound, nothing that was ever done to you is worth giving up eternity in heaven for. Your unforgiveness is not hurting the other person, it is hurting you. Unforgiveness binds you to the pain in your past. You cannot ever pay that person back for what they did to you. Let go and let God. Vengeance is His alone. He alone is qualified to be a judge.

We, as Christians, are commanded to forgive. Regardless of what they did to us. Regardless of what they did to anyone else.

Forgive, not because they deserve forgiveness, but because you deserve peace. – Author Unknown

EPILOGUE

As I publish this study guide, I have been out of the abusive marriage for thirty years. I am living proof it is possible to get free, but that does not mean it is easy.

For decades, I wondered "Why me?" about the abuse. I was so glad when the Lord revealed this curse to me so I finally understand why me.

It is my hope that this study guide will also help you understand why you.

May you walk more free of abuse than you ever have, all the days of your life.

Glynda Lomax
January 2018

ANSWER KEY

Page 8 – The Four Phases Leading Into Abuse

1. Isolation, Elimination of Resources, The Mental Tear-Down, Physical Abuse

Page 12 – Defining Abuse

1. physical

2. ugly words, inside

3. terrorism

4. Verbal, believing, lies

5. sexual

6. Rape

7. financial accounts, assets

8. Legal

9. stalking

Page 20 – The Revelation of the Curse of Abuse

1. open door

3. appropriate

4. Everyone has not appropriated what Jesus did for them and renewed their mind in His Word to overcome their sin.

5. shed Blood of Jesus Christ

Page 23 – Have You Ever Wondered Why You Behave the Way You Do?

1. twisted, crooked, twisted, perverse, crooked

2. male bloodline

3. generational curse

Page 28 – To Deal with Curses You Must Know About Demons

1. demons

2. serpent, devil, Satan

3. Satan

4. devil, angels

5. Word of God

Page 33 – Evidence Suggests that Demons are Fallen Angels

1. Scriptural, abilities

2. Angels

4. conversations

5. belief system, doctrine

Page 37 - Demons have Intelligence

1. Jesus

2. will

3. everything

4. emotions

5. Demons, James 2:19

Page 42 – Demons have Personalities and They Want to Cause Harm

1. identity

2. intelligence, emotions, volition, sense of self

3. harming, harm

4. power

5. allows

6. tame

Page 47 – We are in a Battle

1. insult, claiming

2. knowledge

3. useless

4. destroy, the devil

5. principalities, powers

Page 50 – We have Dominion

1. weapons

2. armour

3. new covenant

4. dominion

5. Jesus also gave that power to the 70 He sent out.

Page 55 – Deliverance didn't End at the Cross

1. power, power, hurt

2. rejoice, rejoice

3. cast out devils, new tongues

4. liar, murderers, destroyer

5. snakes

6. depart

7. bound

8. demons

Page 58 – Are We Delivered of Demons as Soon as We Get Saved?

1. sin, appetites

2. demonic

3. sins, appetites, bad habits

4. power, power

Page 61 – How Demons Gain Access to You

1. sinful thoughts, action

2. us, homes

3. sin

4 mind, renewal

Page 65 – Demons Access Us through Places and Objects

1. territory

2. demons

3. cursed

4. movies

5. images

Page 68 – Special Categories of Objects

1. occult

2. religion

3. Satan

4. Satan

Page 71 – Ways Demons Afflict You

1. attack

2. Witchcraft

3. wound, soul wounds

4. doorways, forgive

5. inwardly

6. concert

7. influence

Page 73 – Authority to Cast Out Demons

1. saved

2. evil spirit

Page 77 – How to Stop Demons from Coming through Soul Tunnels

1. soul ties

2. Matthew 5:28

3. looketh

4. affections, affections

5. Spoken covenants

6. Unforgiveness

Page 87 – What Makes You an Abuse Magnet – A Little Known Spiritual Law About Demons

1. Demons

2. nature

3. sin

4. draw

5. magnet

6. always

NOTES

NOTES